The Best Of Broadway

for
VOCAL DUETS

HAL•LEONARD®
CORPORATION

7777 W. BLUEMOUND RD. P.O. BOX 13819 MILWAUKEE, WI 53213

Memory
(From "CATS")

Soprano and Baritone

Music by ANDREW LLOYD WEBBER
Text by TREVOR NUNN after T.S. ELIOT

lect at my feet_____ And the wind_____ be-gins to moan.

Mem - 'ry._____ All a - lone in the moon - light_____ I can smile at the old days,____ I was beau-ti - ful

Mem - 'ry._____ All a - lone in the moon - light_____ I can smile at the old days,____ I was beau-ti - ful

then._____ I re - mem - ber the time I knew what hap-pi-ness was, Let the

then._____ I re - mem - ber the time I knew what hap-pi-ness was,____ Let the

mem - 'ry live a - gain. Ev' - ry street lamp

mem - 'ry live a - gain. Ev' - ry street lamp

seems to beat___ a fa - tal - is - - tic warn - ing.

seems to beat___ a fa - tal - is - - tic warn - ing.

Some - one mut - ters_ and a street lamp gut - ters_ and soon it will be

Some - one mut - ters_ and a street lamp gut - ters_ and soon it will be

6

Burnt out ends of smo - ky days, _____ the

The street lamp dies an - oth - er

stale cold smell _____ of morn - ing.

touch me you'll un-der-stand what hap-pi-ness is. Look, a

touch me you'll un-der-stand what hap-pi-ness is. Look, a

new day has be - gun.

new day has be - gun.

p

rit.

All At Once You Love Her

(From "PIPE DREAM")

Soprano and Baritone

Words by OSCAR HAMMERSTEIN II
Music by RICHARD RODGERS

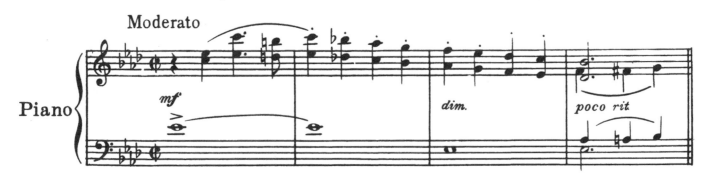

sud - den blare of trum-pets and the rat - tle of drums, A

dream will take pos - ses - sion of your heart.___

Refrain *(slowly, with expression)*

p

Ah,___ Ah,___

mp

You start to light___ her cig - a -

Refrain *(slowly, with expression)*

mp

her. You like her eyes, you tell her
her. You like her eyes, you tell her

so. She thinks you're wise and clev -
so. She thinks you're wise and clev -

er, Ah, Ah,
er, You kiss good - night and then you

You'll kiss good-night for-ev - er.

know You'll kiss good-night for-ev - er.

You won-der where _____ your heart can go Then all at

You won-der where _____ your heart can go Then all at

once you know.

once you know.

13

Sunrise, Sunset
(From the Musical "FIDDLER ON THE ROOF")

Soprano and Baritone

Lyrics by SHELDON HARNICK
Music by JERRY BOCK

Getting To Know You

(From "THE KING AND I")

Soprano and Alto or Baritone

Words by OSCAR HAMMERSTEIN II
Music by RICHARD RODGERS

It's a ver-y an-cient say-ing But a true and hon-est thought, That if

you be-come a teach-er, by your pu-pils you'll be taught.

As a

Get - ting to like you, get - ting to hope you like

Get - ting to like you, get - ting to hope you like

me.

me. Get - ting to know you, Put - ting it my way but

You are pre - cise - ly _____ My cup of

nice - ly, _____

21

22

I Whistle A Happy Tune

(From "THE KING AND I")

Soprano and Alto
or Baritone

Words by OSCAR HAMMERSTEIN II
Music by RICHARD RODGERS

When - ev - er I feel a - fraid   I   hold my head e - rect   And

make be-lieve you are. *(Whistle) _____

You may be as brave as you make be-

lieve you are. _____

*May be omitted

Oh, What A Beautiful Mornin'

(From "OKLAHOMA!)

*Soprano and Alto
or Baritone*

Words by OSCAR HAMMERSTEIN II
Music by RICHARD RODGERS

Refrain

feel - in' Ev - 'ry-thing's go - in' my way.

feel - in' Ev - 'ry - thing's go - in' my way.

feel - in' Ev - 'ry - thing's go - in' my way.

Oh, what a beau - ti - ful day.

Oh, what a beau - ti - ful day.

Oh, what a beau - ti - ful day.

People Will Say We're In Love

(From "OKLAHOMA!")

*Soprano and Alto
or Baritone*

Words by OSCAR HAMMERSTEIN II
Music by RICHARD RODGERS

37

Till the stars fade from a - bove. _____

_mp_

Sweet-heart ___ they're sus - pect - ing things,___ _f_ Peo - ple will

_f_ Peo - ple will

mf espr.

1. say we're in love. _____ 2. love. _____ _mf_

1. 2.

_mf_

The Sound Of Music
(From "THE SOUND OF MUSIC")

Soprano and Baritone

Words by OSCAR HAMMERSTEIN II
Music by RICHARD RODGERS

beat like the wings of the birds that rise from the lake to the

trees.

My heart wants to sigh like a chime that flies from a church on a

To laugh like a brook that falls o-ver

breeze, To laugh like a brook when it trips and falls o-ver

44

Climb Ev'ry Mountain
(From "THE SOUND OF MUSIC")

Soprano and Baritone

Words by OSCAR HAMMERSTEIN II
Music by RICHARD RODGERS

48

49

My Favorite Things
(From "THE SOUND OF MUSIC")

Soprano and Baritone

Words by OSCAR HAMMERSTEIN II
Music by RICHARD RODGERS

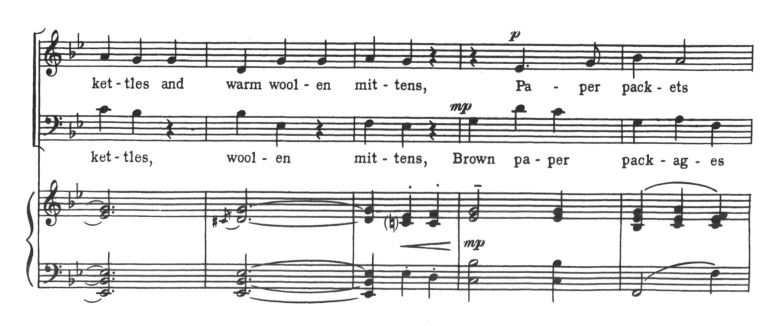

52

It Might As Well Be Spring

(From "STATE FAIR")

Words by OSCAR HAMMERSTEIN II
Music by RICHARD RODGERS

Soprano and Baritone

tend-ing I am won-der-ful and know-ing I'm a dope.

Refrain (*gracefully*)

I'm as rest-less as a wil-low in a wind-storm, I'm as

I'm as rest-less as a wil-low in a wind-storm,

Refrain (*gracefully*)

jump-y as a pup-pet on a string.

I'd say that you had spring fe-ver, But I

Hear- ing words that I have nev - er heard from a man I've yet to

street,

meet. I'm as

I'm as bus - y as a spi - der spin - ning day dreams;

gid - dy as a ba - by on a swing. I have - n't seen a cro - cus or a

I have - n't seen a cro - cus or a

It's A Grand Night For Singing
(From "STATE FAIR")

Soprano and Baritone

Words by OSCAR HAMMERSTEIN II
Music by RICHARD RODGERS

61

62

* *Second time use small notes and "forte"*

64